Traditional Wagashi with a Twist Cookbook

Delicious Wagashi Recipes That Will Transport You to Asia

BY

Stephanie Sharp

Copyright © 2020 by Stephanie Sharp

License Notes

WWWWWWWWWWWWWWWWWWWWWWWWWWWWWWWWWWWW

Table of Contents

Introduction

From wagashi cookies to Tofu Panna Cotta, cooks at home will be transformed by the recipes in Wagashi Cookbook dedicated to Japanese treats popularly known as wagashi. By tradition, wagashi is served as part of the tea ceremony, but it has found its place in contemporary cuisines as elegant desserts that are light and beautifully crafted.

Dated back centuries, this art form is often found to be quite intriguing, and Wagashi Cookbook has transformed traditional dishes and techniques of Japan's wagashi masters in order to suit modern audiences. With the simple instructions, anyone can have wagashi ready in minutes from the patented microwave pot.

Wagashi, from various rice flours, are low in sugar and gluten free. Inspired by the distinctive qualities of each season and nature's beauty, wagashi mirrors the world naturally in color and form. Get started and intrigue your guests today!

Soft Wagashi Cookie

This is a very traditional confection in Japan. It is made with rice flour and bean jam, and it is SO tasty! Some cooks add a bit of egg, too.

Serves: 24

Time: 25 minutes

Ingredients:

- Matcha green tea leaves (2 tsp)
- baking powder (3/4 oz)
- rice flour (1 oz, Joshin ko)
- Shiro An (10 ½ oz)

Directions:

1. Mix baking powder into the rice flour. Add mixture into the white bean paste. Combine well. Divide into two portions.

2. Dissolve Matcha powder into a bit of water. Mix that into 1/2 of dough. Wrap it using a paper towel to drain the water.

3. Divide plain dough into six sections. Repeat process for the Matcha dough.

Make flowers using plain and Matcha dough. Place them on microwave safe baking tray with baking paper.

4. Heat for 1 ½ to 2 minutes at 500 watts in microwave.

Allow them to cool in oven and then remove them. Serve.

Water Peony Confection – Mizubotan

This cake is tailor-made to serve during summer tea ceremonies. The lightness of the confection provides you with a feeling of coolness.

Serves: 20-24

Time: 1 hour 5 minutes

Ingredients:

- bean paste (16 ½ oz, smooth, pink koshian)
- water (1 ½ cups)
- sugar (7 oz, granulated)
- kudzu (3 ½ oz)
- sweet bean paste (as needed)

Directions:

1. Prepare the pink koshian balls. These will form the middle of the confections.

2. Dissolve kudzu into water until no more lumps remain.

Place kudzu and water in heavy-bottom pot. Mix sugar into it.

3. Cook on low to medium heat. Stir continuously until mixture becomes thicker and starts to appear clearer.

4. When mixture is clear, remove from heat. Place in pan of hot water, so the mixture won't harden.

5. Take some of heated kudzu (about an oz) then place on the tips of your fingers.

6. Place one ball on top of kudzu. Turn it upside down. Form kudzu around the ball. Pinch kudzu and enclose the ball with it. Do the same process with the rest of the heated kudzu.

7. Place in preheated steamer with a cloth liner. Steam on med-high for about five minutes. Remove from steamer. Allow to cool. Serve when cooled.

Kabocha Soymilk Zenzai

Not many desserts are healthy and vegan-friendly, but this one is. It is made from kabocha squash cooked in red bean soup and soymilk.

Serves: 12

Time: 4 minutes

Ingredients:

- water (1 ½ cup, filtered)
- rice flour (2 cups, shiratamako)
- syrup (4 tbsp, maple)
- soymilk (8 cups)
- squash (1, preferably kabocha)

Directions:

1. Combine the water and rice flour. Boil for a couple minutes, creating the rice flour dumplings, allow them to cool.

2. Remove kabocha seeds and peel their skins then cut into tiny pieces.

3. Combine the kabocha, maple syrup and soymilk into a pan. Cook for about 15 minutes on medium heat.

4. Transfer mixture into a food processor. Blend and strain it.

5. Place kabocha mixture with dumplings into containers. Top using cooked azuki beans. Serve.

Warabi Mochi

This tasty treat is made from bracken starch, also called warabi starch. Warabi is a Japanese fern, and the starch comes from the underground stems. The texture is more jelly-like than other mochi, made with glutinous rice.

Serves: 8

Time: 35 minutes

Ingredients:

- water (3 ½ cups, filtered)
- sugar (1 cup, granulated)
- jelly-consistency confection (1 ½ cups)

For toppings:

- Syrup
- brown sugar (kuromitsu)
- soy bean flour (1/2 cup, kinako)

Directions:

1. Sprinkle soybean flour onto cookie sheet.

2. Combine warabi mochi, water and sugar into medium sized saucepan. Combine well.

3. Heat mixture on medium heat until it begins to boil. Reduce heat.

4. Stir vigorously with a spatula for about 10 minutes. Mixture should become translucent and thick.

5. Remove mochi from heat. Transfer to pre-floured cookie sheet. Sprinkle additional flour on the top of mochi. Allow to cool in your fridge for about 20 minutes.

6. Once mochi cools, remove from refrigerator. Slice into cubes of 3/4 inch.

7. Toss warabi mochi with flour. Serve on plate. Pour syrup on top if you desire.

Walnut-Fig Yokan

This treat was born when a cook was asked to create a type of wagashi that people could eat with bread. It's a dried fruit yokan, and the other ingredients work well with it, including red bean paste, brown sugar, figs and walnuts.

Serves: 12

Time: 45 minutes

Ingredients:

- walnuts (5 oz)
- rum (10 tbsp)
- figs (9 oz., dried)
- salt (1 tsp, kosher)
- sugar (4 cups, granulated)
- sweet bean paste (1/2 lb.,)
- gelatin (1 pkg., powdered, kanten)
- water (1 ¼ cups, filtered)

Directions:

1. Chop figs then simmer them in rum until figs have absorbed it all and have become soft. You can add some water if needed.

2. Toast walnuts for 8 minutes at 350 degrees F then chop them up.

3. Add gelatin to cold, filtered water then stir until gelatin dissolves.

4. Add the sweet bean paste, salt and sugar.

5. Continue to cook until consistency is pourable but thick.

6. Add the walnuts and figs, as desired.

7. Pour mixture into the molds and allow to cool down at room temperature. Serve.

Fruit Cream Anmitsu

This type of anmitsu starts with agar jelly cubes, made from a red algae. The agar (gelatin) will be dissolved in water to create jelly. You can serve it in a small bowl with various fruits and sweet azuki bean paste.

Serves: 8

Time: 1 hour 50 minutes

Ingredients:

- sweet bean paste (1 cup)

For the kanten jelly:

- water (1 ½ cups, filtered)
- sugar (4 tbsp, granulated)
- gelatin powder (1 tsp)

For the dark syrup (Kuromitsu):

- ice cream (3 ½ cups)
- water (4 tbsp, filtered)
- sugar (8 tbsp, brown)
- corn syrup (6 tbsp, light)

Directions:

1. Combine gelatin powder, sugar and water to a medium pan to make kanten jelly.

2. Cook on medium heat until it has reached boiling then lower heat. Stir continuously as you allow to simmer for a couple minutes.

3. Pour mixture into mold then refrigerate for about an hour until it sets up.

4. Combine dark syrup ingredients. Stir them well and place in microwave. When mixture starts boiling, remove it and stir once more. Set aside and allow to cool.

5. Cut kanten jelly into small cubes. Place in four individual bowls. Place ice cream and your choice of fruits over the top. Drizzle with dark syrup. Serve.

Sweet Potatoes Chestnuts – Kuri Kinton

This is a sweet concoction that starts with candied chestnuts and Japanese sweet potatoes. It is served traditionally on New Year's, but it can be made anytime. The chestnuts have an intense flavor that goes so well with the native sweet potatoes of Japan.

Serves: 12-16

Time: 8 hours 40 minutes including 8 hours soaking time

Ingredients:

- salt (2/3 tsp, kosher)
- chestnuts (2 jars, candied, Marrons Glacés)
- mirin (6 tbsp)
- sugar (7 ¾ oz, granulated)
- Japanese sweet potatoes (2 ¼ lbs., satsuma-imo)

Directions:

1. Peel sweet potatoes and cut them into 1/2" circles. Soak into bowl of water for approximately 8 hours.

2. Place sweet potatoes into a large pot. Cover them using water and bring them to boil.

3. Lower the heat and simmer until you can pierce potatoes with ease using a toothpick. Drain and reserve the water.

4. Add 1/3 of sugar. Mash until potatoes are smooth. Add cooking liquid if you need it.

5. Add the rest of the chestnut syrup, sugar and salt as desired. Add liquid from the pot until mixture is the consistency of cream soup.

6. Continue to cook over medium -high heat until you can run a spatula along the skillet bottom and a channel remains there.

7. Add Marrons Glacés. Heat well and add more syrup if you wish. It should be quite sweet and taste like chestnuts. Transfer to a bowl and set aside. Serve.

Tofu Panna Cotta

How about a dessert delicacy made with tofu? This doesn't happen often. Tofu is transformed amazingly into a dessert with this special recipe. It's even vegan-friendly.

Serves: 8

Time: 25 minutes

Ingredients:

- gelatin powder (1 tsp)
- lemon juice (2 tsp)
- soymilk (2/3 cup)
- tofu (1 cup, soft)
- syrup maple (1 cup)

Directions:

1. Warm tofu into microwave oven for approximately 1 minute.

2. Combine ingredients except the tofu in pan. Bring to boil.

3. Place tofu and contents from step 2 then combine well.

4. Pour tofu mixture into serving dish then place into fridge to chill and then harden.

5. Use marmalade to garnish and serve.

Matcha Jelly

This is an absolutely unbeatable dessert that combines the sweetness of condensed milk and sugar with Matcha's bitter green tea taste.

Serves: 4

Time: 15 minutes

Ingredients:

- potato starch (2 tsp)
- gelatin (1 tsp, powdered)
- sugar (2 tbsp, granulated)
- Matcha green tea (2 tsp, powdered)
- Condensed milk (as desired)

Directions:

1. Combine the sugar and tea powder into a bowl. Mix well.

2. Combine 6 ¾ fluid ounces of water with the gelatin and potato starch into a small pot. Mix well.

3. Heat on medium high and stir. When it reaches a boil, lower heat and allow to simmer for a couple minutes.

4. Pour contents of the bowl from step 1 in the pot from step 2. Mix them together.

5. Pour mixture through the strainer into a container. Place that container onto an ice tray to set and cool.

6. Once it has set, cut into small pieces and arrange them on serving dish. Pour condensed milk on top and serve.

Triangle Rice Cake with Sweet Beans - Minazuki

The triangle shape of these confections is representative of pieces of ice in the summer. It was once important, before freezers were common. In the city of Kyoto, this dessert is served on the 30th of June, as a ritual of prayer for good health.

Serves: 8

Time: 25 minutes

Ingredients:

- sweet beans (1 cup, sweet, amanatto, simmered)
- water (2 cups, filtered)
- sugar (7 tbsp, granulated)
- corn starch (2 tbsp)
- flour (1 cup, wheat)

Directions:

1. Mix the sugar, flour and corn starch using a whisk. Add the filtered water until they completely dissolve.

2. In a heat resistant container pour in about 90% of flour mixture. Cover with cling wrap. Microwave for about three minutes.

3. Uncover container. Spread the sweet bean paste over the whole surface evenly then pour the remainder of the flour mixture on top of bean paste.

4. Cover using the cling wrap again. Microwave for a couple minutes then allow to cool. Slice and serve.

Agar Plum Wine Jelly

Don't be w orried that the wine will make this dessert unsuitable for children. That would be a shame. The alcohol actually burns off in the prep stage. The agar jelly offers a tempting plum scent, and kids and adults love this dessert.

Serves: 8

Time: 1/2 hour

Ingredients:

- ume plums (4, chopped)
- sugar (2 tbsp)
- gelatin powder (4 tsp, agar)
- plum wine (4 cups, umeshu)

Directions:

1. Combine the sugar and the gelation into the container. Mix and mash together.

2. Pour the plum wine into the saucepan then boil for approximately 2 minutes. This burns off alcohol.

3. Mix step 1 ingredients with the plum wine hen bring back up to boil.

4. Evenly divide the plum (chopped) into four small containers.

5. Pour the contents from step 3 into all containers, over the tops of the plums then chill into your refrigerator.

6. Serve.

Glutinous Cherry Rice Cakes - Sakura Mochigome Mochi

Sakura mochi is wagashi made from sweet rice, which is also known as glutinous rice in the form of sweet pink mochi. It is generally filled with some type of sweet tasting bean paste, and then wrapped up in pickled cherry leaves.

Serves: 8

Time: 35 minutes

Ingredients:

- cherry leaves (8, pickled)
- food coloring (dash, red)
- rice (2 cups, sweet)
- bean paste (strained, koshian, as desired)

Directions:

1. Cook the sweet rice and food coloring.

2. Shape bean paste into four balls approximately 1 ¼ in diameter. Set them aside.

3. Pound the sweet rice using a rolling pin. Leave it a bit grainy.

4. After rice cools, divide into four portions of the same size. Place one into your hand. Put one ball of the bean paste in the middle then mold rice around the bean paste.

5. Wrap all balls with cherry leaves. Serve.

Rice Dumplings Sweet Sauce – Mitarashi Dango

In this recipe, mochi balls are browned on a grill, then poured over with a soy sauce-based sweet sauce. There is a savory smell and salty taste, which match so well with the remainder of the sugary sauce. This dango recipe is easy to make.

Serves: 48 confections (16 skewers)

Time: 90 minutes

Ingredients:

For the dumplings:

- water (1 ½ cup, warm)
- rice flour (4 ¼ oz, mochiko)
- rice flour (10 oz., jyoshinko)

For the sauce:

- soy sauce (2 2/3 tbsp, thin, usukuchi shoyu)
- arrowroot/potato starch (2 tbsp., katakuriko)
- water (10 2/3 tbsp, filtered)
- sugar (8 tbsp, dark brown)

Directions:

1. To create sauce: Mix sauce ingredients into heavy pan until arrowroot/potato starch has dissolved. Cook on medium-low heat until starch is dissolved, then thick.

2. To create dumplings: mix both the flours together. Sift into a medium bowl. Add water. Mix until it forms a dough. Knead dough until smooth.

3. Separate the dough into pieces (1/2 ounce each). Form dough into small sized balls.

4. Thread three balls onto pre-soaked bamboo skewers then steam skewers for about 15 minutes on medium-high in a steamer lined in cloth until they have cooked through. Grill skewered dumplings on high until lightly browned.

5. Brush the sweet sauce on the dumpling tops before you serve them.

Rice Cakes in Oak Leaves – Kashiwa Mochi

This wagashi is traditionally served every May 5th, which is Children's Day in Japan. It is made with rice flour and non-glutinous rice. It has a chewier texture than most other desserts, and the taste is lightly sweet.

Serves: 12

Time: 1 hour

Ingredients:

- water (1 ½ cups, filtered)
- glutinous rice (2 cups, joshinko)
- rice flour (1/2 cup, refined, shiratamako)
- Potato starch (if needed)
- bean paste (strained, koshian, as needed)
- oak leaves (12 large)

Directions:

1. Mix the water, rice flour and glutinous rice then knead until dough mixture becomes soft.

2. Steam dough for approximately 20 minutes in a heated steamer.

3. Remove dough from the steamer then allow to cool, knead well.

4. Divide dough into 6 round balls of equal sizes. Spread into oval shapes using rolling pin.

5. Place bean paste into the center of dough pieces. Wrap all using oak leaves, 1 each.

Matcha Caramel Pudding

This recipe will create a beautiful serving.

Serves: 6

Time: 90 minutes

Ingredients:

For the Matcha pudding:

- cream (6 ¾ fl. oz., heavy)
- milk (10 ¼ fl. oz., whole)
- green tea powder (1 tbsp.,)
- egg (2 yolks., large)
- sugar (5 tbsp., granulated)
- eggs (3, large)
- Vanilla extract (pure)
- water (2 tbsp, warm)

For the caramel:

- sugar (5 tbsp., granulated)

Directions:

1. Heat the sugar into a fry pan until caramelized and browned. Transfer it to the bottom of a heat-safe container then beat the whole eggs into a bowl.

2. Add the egg yolks and sugar then continue beating.

3. In another bowl, use the hot water to dissolve the Matcha green tea powder. Add to egg mixture and combine. Add the cream and milk then beat them together.

4. Add the vanilla extract then strain mixture using a strainer, pouring into the heat-safe container.

5. Place chopsticks across the top of oven tray then place pudding container on top of them. Pour some hot water into the tray.

6. Preheat oven to 325 degrees F. Bake mixture for approximately 45 minutes.

7. When it is cool enough to be handled, transfer pudding container to the refrigerator for cooling. Slice then serve.

Sweet Rice Balls – Ohagi

Ohagi, or sweet rice balls, are generally made from glutinous rice. They are often eaten during the spring and autumn seasons, for Buddhist holidays. The name ohagi comes from an autumn flower, called the bush clover, or hagi.

Serves: 24

Time: 50 minutes

Ingredients:

- soy bean flour (12 tbsp, kinako)
- bean paste (5 cups, sweet)
- salt (1/2 tsp., kosher)
- rice (2 cups., sweet., mochigome)
- rice (2 cups., white., uruchi mai)

Directions:

1. Mix the rice together thoroughly and prepare them following the usual procedures you would do for any other rice.

2. Remove hot rice and place into sturdy bowl. Add salt. Vigorously mix using a spoon.

3. Wet your hands then pinch a golf ball sized dough piece. Flatten into your palm and place a spoonful of the bean paste into the middle of dough.

4. Pinch sides of dough and encase paste. Dip into the powdered soy bean flour. Serve.

Mini Sweet Bean Sandwiches – Dorayaki

This is a very classic confection in Japan. It is made with a honey pancake on top and bottom, and a filling made from sweet red beans. It is a very popular dessert among both adults and children.

Serves: 30

Time: 1 hour

Ingredients:

- sugar (5 ½ oz., granulated)
- eggs (4, large)
- water (3 1/3 fl., oz)
- honey (2 tbsp.,)
- bean paste with skins (21 oz.,)
- baking soda (1 tsp)
- flour (8 ½ o., plain)
- Vegetable oil

Directions:

1. Beat the eggs into a medium sized bowl. Add the sugar. Use a whisk to mix them together thoroughly.

2. Add the honey and water. Combine well.

3. Mix the baking soda with the plain flour. Sprinkle in. Mix until flour is integrated completely.

4. When the batter appears smooth, cover it with cling wrap. Refrigerate for 1/2 hour.

5. Heat fry pan on low heat and coat thinly with veggie oil.

6. Add 1 tbsp. of batter to fry pan, make circles with a diameter of roughly 2 1/3 inches.

7. When bubbles start breaking the surface of the batter top, turn pancakes over after edges are dry.

8. Cook for another minute. Repeat until you have made 60 pancakes then allow to cool.

9. Place the bean paste on top of a pancake thickly then press another pancake on top, creating a sandwich. Repeat process for the rest of the pancakes. Serve.

Plum Perilla Confection - Ume Shiso Sanshoku Dango

Dango is a term used to describe mochi dumplings that are ball-shaped and small. The mochi does not need to be sweetened, since the sauces and toppings are. Dango are sometimes served on bamboo sticks, making them easier to eat.

Serves: 9

Time: 45 minutes

Ingredients:

- perilla (8, chopped, green, shiso)
- plum (4, chopped, pickled, umeboshi)
- water (1 ½ cups, filtered)
- flour (2 cups, dango)

Directions:

1. Combine the water along with the flour then knead thoroughly by hand.

2. Divide the dough into three equal pieces.

3. Mix the plum pieces (chopped) into one dough piece. Mix the shiso leaves (chopped) in another piece. Leave the third piece of the dough plain.

4. Shape portions into bite sized dough balls. Boil in the heated water for approximately 2-3 minutes.

5. Drain the hot water. Allow to cool. Slide three different colored, cooked dough balls onto each skewer. Serve by skewer.

Grilled Kudzu – Grilled Kuzu

Kudzu is known as kuzu in Japan, and it is even more revered than is ginseng in the country. The roots are the plant's potent energy points. The Japanese people use roots in cooking and in medicine, as well.

Serves: 26-36

Time: 2 hours

Ingredients:

- bean paste (12 oz., red, koshian, smooth)
- kudzu (8 ½ oz., kuzu)
- sugar (10 oz., granulated)
- water (4 2/3 cups., filtered)
- Potato starch (katakuriko)

Directions:

1. Dissolve kudzu in water until all lumps have completely dissolved then train.

2. Place the liquid into a heavy pot. Mix in the sugar. Cook on medium-low heat then stir continuously until mixture is ½ cooked and thickened.

3. Mix in the bean paste. Continue cooking and stirring until ingredients are all thoroughly blended. Remove from heat. Pour in a coldwater rinsed 7x7" lined mold.

4. Place mold into a cloth-lined, pre-heated steamer. Place a towel under the steamer lid. Steam on medium-high for about 45 minutes to an hour.

5. Remove the steamer then set on wire rack to cool. After about a half-hour cooling time, place the cling wrap on the surface of kudzu, so it won't dry out.

6. Once kudzu has cooled, unmold and cut into pieces. Dust each side carefully using potato starch.

7. In a heated nonstick pan, grill all sides of kudzu until browned lightly. Cool down to room temperature. Serve.

Kudzu Asuki Beans Dumplings - Kuzu Manju Dumplings

Kudzu root starch is created from the kudzu plant. It's a member of the bean family. When the powder is heated, it thickens, which means it's a valuable and useful addition to drinks, sweets and other recipes.

Serves: may vary

Time: 25 minutes

Ingredients:

- azuki bean paste (7 oz., store bought, w/skins)
- sugar (3 ½ oz, granulated)
- water (6 ¾ fl., oz, filtered)
- kudzu root starch (1 ¾ oz)

Directions:

Combine the kudzu root starch with 2/3 of the water into a medium sized bowl. Mix well until fully dissolved. Pour through strainer into a large pot.

2. Dissolve the kudzu starch from what was left in bowl with the remaining 1/3 of water. Pour through the strainer and into same pot.

3. Add the sugar to the pot. Stir and combine. Heat on medium-high. Stir mixture until sugar completely dissolves.

4. You will notice that transparent clumps start forming. When 60% of the total mixture is clumpy begin to add bean paste. Mix well.

5. Reduce heat to medium-low then knead or stir until all contents are transparent.

6. Use moistened soup spoon and drop balls of the mixture from the pot onto middle of a flat piece of cling wrap. They should be roughly the size of tennis balls.

7. Bring the edges of wrap together and tie using string. Allow to rest on counter until they set. Chill in fridge for 1/2 hour. Remove cling wrap. Serve.

Jelly Cubes with Bean Paste Fruit

There isn't one set way you have to use when you create yours. Feel free to add ice cream or fruit on top when you serve.

Serves: 12

Time: 1 3/4 hours

Ingredients:

- bean paste (2 cups)
- sugar (6 tbsp., granulated)
- water (4 cups., filtered)
- gelatin powder (1/4 oz., kanten/agar)
- Fresh or canned fruit, if desired

For kuromitsu (dark syrup):

- water (1/2 cup., filtered)
- sugar (1 cup., light brown)

Directions:

1. To prepare the syrup, place the water and light brown sugar into a pot. Bring to a boil on high heat setting. Boil for about a minute and turn heat off. Allow syrup to cool down.

2. Use water to dissolve gelatin powder. Heat mixture on medium. heat and stir with wooden ladle. When liquid boils, lower heat. Simmer for a couple minutes.

3. Add the sugar to gelatin mixture. Bring to boil. Remove pot from the stove.

4. Pour liquid gelatin into a rectangle-shaped mold. Allow to cool in your fridge for an hour or longer.

5. Remove hardened gelatin from mold. Cut into little cubes.

6. Place jelly cubes in serving bowl. Add bean paste and sliced fruit. Pour syrup on top. Serve.

Kabocha Soymilk Zenzai

Here is a healthy type of dessert, suitable even for vegans. It's made with kabocha squash that are cooked with red bean soup and soymilk, for a truly unique taste.

Serves: 6

Time: 45 minutes

Ingredients:

- water (3/4., filtered)
- flour (1 cup., rice)
- maple syrup (2 tbsp)
- milk (4 cups., soy)
- kabocha squash (1/2)
- Azuki beans (cooked, as needed)

Directions:

1. Combine the rice flour and water and boil for two to three minutes to make dumplings. Allow them to cool.

2. Remove seeds from the squash and peel skin. Cut squash into small sized pieces.

3. Combine squash, maple syrup and soymilk into the pan. Cook for about 15 minutes on medium. heat.

4. Transfer mixture to a food processor. Blend well and strain.

5. Serve the squash mixture with dumplings and azuki beans.

Perilla Plum Wagashi

This perilla and plum confection is made from mochi dumplings. They will be skewered onto bamboo sticks that are fun and easy to eat with. The plum is used to evoke the green colors of spring and the perilla adds a mild fragrance.

Serves: 4

Time: 45 minutes

Ingredients:

- perilla (4, chopped, green)
- plum, (2 pcs., chopped., pickled)
- water (3/4 cup., filtered)
- flour (1 cup)

Directions:

1. Combine the water and flour then knead well by hand.

2. Divide dough into three equal parts then mix the chopped pickled plums into 1/3 and repeat process with the chopped perilla leaves. Blend into dough evenly. Leave 1/3 of dough plain.

3. Shape the dough portions into bite-size balls (mochi). Boil into water for about two or three minutes.

4. Drain hot water then allow the balls to cool. Slide three balls of different colors onto each skewer and serve.

Sugar Coated Sweet Potato Fries

This confection brings back memories to the people in Japan who enjoy it. You can make it easily with even leftover sweet potatoes.

Serves: 4

Time: 35 minutes

Ingredients:

- water (1/2 cup., filtered)
- sugar (1 cup., granulated)
- Salad oil to fry with
- potatoes (2, sweet)
- sesame (1 dash, black)

Directions:

1. Your first step is to Julienne the sweet potatoes then heat the salad oil on low heat in a medium sized pan.

2. Fry the strips of sweet potato until crispy and no longer moist.

3. Combine the water and sugar in another pan and cook until mixture has thickened.

4. Mix in the sweet potato strips. Sprinkle the black sesame on top and serve.

Strawberry Mugwort Rice Cake

This amazing rice cake is colored with flowers, fruits or plants like gardenia, mugwort or strawberries. If the dough seems too wet, you can add extra rice flour, which will make it easier to handle.

Serves: 4

Time: 3/4 hour

Ingredients:

- strawberries (4, strawberries, hulls removed)
- mugwort (1/2 tbsp., dried)
- sugar (1/2 cup, granulated)
- rice flour (1/4 cup)
- water (1/2 cup., filtered)
- Potato starch (as desired)
- Bean paste, strained (as desired)

Directions:

1. Cover the strawberries using a layer of bean paste. Mold them into balls.

2. Combine the mugwort, sugar, water and flour into a bowl. Combine well.

3. Transfer mixture to a heat-safe container. Heat into the microwave for approximately 1 minute. Mix well.

4. Repeat step 3 until the dough is transparent and bouncy. This may take 2-3 times.

5. Sprinkle the dough using starch. Spread on tray.

6. After the dough has cooled, cut into eight pieces, all equal sizes. Wrap each ball into dough piece. Serve.

Water Steamed Bun Manju Dessert

This Japanese dessert, known as manju, consists of cake that is normally made from rice powder or flour, stuffed with sweet bean paste.

Serves: 12

Time: 1 hour 40 minutes including 1-hour chilling time

Ingredients:

- starch (1/4 cup, kudzu)
- sugar (1/3 cup, granulated)
- water (1 cup., filtered)
- Azuki bean paste (smooth)

Directions:

1. Divide the bean paste into 12 equal parts then shape them into balls.

2. Combine the starch and water. After starch has dissolved, add the sugar and stir.

3. Place step 2 mixture into a saucepan. Heat on medium until dough looks transparent, while constantly stirring. Do not allow the mixture to burn.

4. Pour 1/2 dough into the dampened mold. Bury bean paste into the middle of dough. Pour the rest of the dough over bean paste balls and cover them.

5. Cool in the refrigerator for approximately 1 hour. Serve.

Soft Wagashi

This is a great recipe that makes a confection like a soft cookie. It will seem more familiar to Western taste. It is made with rice flour and bean jam, and some cooks add a bit of egg, too.

Serves: 12

Time: 1 hour 20 minutes

Ingredients:

- Matcha green tea (1/2- 1 tsp)
- baking powder (1/4 tsp)
- rice flour (1/2 oz)
- bean paste (5 1/3 oz., white, with sugar)

Directions:

1. Mix the baking powder into the flour then add into the bean paste. Combine well and divide into two pieces.

2. Dissolve the Matcha powder into a bit of water then mix Matcha/water and ½ of dough. Wrap into paper towel to absorb the water.

3. Divide one plain dough portion into six parts. Divide the Matcha dough in six parts, as well.

4. Use plain and Matcha dough to make flowers. Place onto a baking tray of your microwave, lined with baking parchment.

5. Heat at 500 watts for one to two minutes in microwave. Remove and serve.

Chestnut Puree Wagashi

This wagashi is made with chestnut puree and flour. The sweets are made in the shape of flowers. The dough is a darker brown than usual, so be patient if you try to color it.

Serves: 14

Time: 1 hour 15 minutes including 1/2-hour chilling time

Ingredients:

- flour (1 ¼ oz., plain)
- sugar (1 ¾ oz., granulated)
- chestnut puree (3 ½ oz)
- Food coloring, as desired

Directions:

1. To create the chestnut dough, mix the chestnut puree and sugar. Wrap into a paper towel.

2. Wring the mixture. Wrap into a new paper towel to absorb liquid. Add 1 ¼ oz. of flour after draining.

3. Mix together then wrap with a cotton cloth. Place into steamer and steam for about 15 minutes.

4. Knead dough to smooth then wrap using cling wrap. Allow to cool. Place into the refrigerator for 1/2 hour.

5. To create gazania wagashi, divide dough into parts. Color them. Create shape of flower from dough pieces. Serve.

Figs Cooked in Ginger Honey and Lemon

Have you ever had figs in a dessert? If not, this is a great recipe to try. The figs in this dessert are roasted with lemon zest, ginger, honey and brown sugar. The result is a bold and wonderful wagashi.

Serves: 4

Time: 35 minutes

Ingredients:

- ginger (10 slices)
- lemon juice (4 tsp)
- honey (6 tbsp., pure)
- water (4 cups., filtered)
- figs (12, whole)

Directions:

1. Use water to lightly wash the figs.

2. Combine all other ingredients into a saucepan and bring to boil.

3. Add the figs and cook on low heat for about 20 minutes. Cool. Serve.

Plum Wine Agar Jelly

The agar jelly in this dessert gives off a refreshing plumb scent. The plum is called "ume" in Japan. Children may enjoy this treat too, since the alcohol burns off during its preparation.

Serves: 2

Time: 35 minutes

Ingredients:

- plum (1, chopped)
- sugar (1/2 tbsp., granulated)
- agar powder (1 tsp)
- plum wine (1 cup)

Directions:

1. Combine the sugar and the agar in a container. Mix and mash.

2. Pour the plum wine into a saucepan then bowl for approximately two minutes. This will burn the alcohol off.

3. Mix the ingredients of steps 1 and 2 then bring to boil once more.

4. Divide the plum into four pieces, evenly.

5. Pour the contents of step 3 over the plums then chill into the refrigerator. Serve.

Conclusion

Thank you so much for holding with me to the very end of this Traditional Wagashi With A Twist Cookbook. I hope you enjoyed all the 30 Delicious Wagashi Recipes That Will Transport You to Asia.

If you enjoyed what you read through, I would really appreciate if you could leave a review on amazon. This will not only assist me in improving on my skills as a recipe writer as well as provide you with more valuable content.

Cheers!

About the Author

Born in New Germantown, Pennsylvania, Stephanie Sharp received a Masters degree from Penn State in English Literature. Driven by her passion to create culinary masterpieces, she applied and was accepted to The International Culinary School of the Art Institute where she excelled in French cuisine. She has married her cooking skills with an aptitude for business by opening her own small cooking school where she teaches students of all ages.

Stephanie's talents extend to being an author as well and she has written over 400 e-books on the art of cooking and baking that include her most popular recipes.

Sharp has been fortunate enough to raise a family near her hometown in Pennsylvania where she, her husband and children live in a beautiful rustic house on an extensive piece of land. Her other passion is taking care of the furry members of her family which include 3 cats, 2 dogs and a potbelly pig named Wilbur.

Watch for more amazing books by Stephanie Sharp coming out in the next few months.

Author's Afterthoughts

I am truly grateful to you for taking the time to read my book. I cherish all of my readers! Thanks ever so much to each of my cherished readers for investing the time to read this book!

With so many options available to you, your choice to buy my book is an honour, so my heartfelt thanks at reading it from beginning to end!

I value your feedback, so please take a moment to submit an honest and open review on Amazon so I can get valuable insight into my readers' opinions and others can benefit from your experience.

Thank you for taking the time to review!

Stephanie   **Sharp**

For announcements about new releases, please

follow my author page on Amazon.com!

You can find that at:

https://www.amazon.com/author/stephanie-sharp

*or Scan **QR-code** below.*